LIFE IS ABOUT CHOICES

LIFE IS ABOUT CHOICES

Creating Our Reality

Ed Scott

iUniverse, Inc.
New York Bloomington

iUniverse books may be ordered through booksellers or by contacting:

iUniverse
1663 Liberty Drive
Bloomington, IN 47403
www.iuniverse.com
1-800-Authors (1-800-288-4677)

Because of the dynamic nature of the Internet, any Web addresses or links contained in this
book may have changed since publication and may no longer be valid. The views expressed
in this work are solely those of the author and do not necessarily reflect the views of the
publisher, and the publisher hereby disclaims any responsibility for them.

ISBN: 978-1-4401-7421-6 (sc)
ISBN: 978-1-4401-7423-0 (hc)
ISBN: 978-1-4401-7422-3 (ebook)

Printed in the United States of America

iUniverse rev. date: 09/25/09

Also by Ed Scott

Wisdom of the Heart:
Create Your Own Reality

CONTENTS

Preface

Stop for a moment and think about the many choices that you make in the course of a single day. Consider the consequences of those choices. Are you simply a bystander, watching your life events unfold in a random fashion? Or do you recognize and make deliberate choices? Life is a continuous series of choices in our wakeful state of being. Knowingly, or otherwise, we design our destiny with our thoughts and our choices. Our casual thoughts and choices are equally as important as those choices made with deliberate intent because both have an energy that attracts our life events.

In a world faced with growing problems in every facet of our daily lives, more and more people are searching for meaningful purpose and happiness in their lives. At some time in our lives, each of us will likely conclude that there must be more to life—there is something missing from our everyday, physical existence. This sense of longing can be the beginning of the discovery of our true being and purpose in our lives. When we learn to trust the synchronicity in our universe, our human intuition and awareness can bring us to a new reality—an experience supported by both religion and science. This discovery of our true identity is part of a spiritual awakening that is now occurring worldwide involving many thousands of people.

We are truly spiritual beings experiencing our unique and separate roles in the drama of life. The extent to which we can create our new reality will depend upon our level of awareness and our commitment to making the right choices throughout our lives. When we are sincere in our commitment to bringing change in our lives, coincidence will bring to us the opportunities and the necessary resources. It is through this process that we find love and beauty to be the ultimate truth of our existence.

For many years, I have studied comparative religion, esoteric writings, philosophy, metaphysics, and other supportive sciences. My travels throughout North America, Europe, and the African continent have provided me an invaluable experience in observing various cultures, values, and belief systems.

In 1984, I was asked to assume the position of board president in the Institute for the Study of Human Awareness in

Minneapolis, Minnesota. Having served in that capacity for fifteen years, I had the opportunity to learn more about human awareness, consciousness, and our unique relationship with the creative force of the universe.

As a police officer in the Minneapolis Police Department, I began my writing experience by drafting policy and procedural directives in 1985. My writing skills were also useful in developing written accreditation standards for the police department manual. That year, I wrote and published *Photo Poems*, my first book of philosophic verses illustrated with my photographs.

My awareness of an evolving worldwide spiritual resurgence prompted me to begin to assist others in their spiritual quest. I then wrote and published *Wisdom of the Heart: Create Your Own Reality*, in 2008.

In publishing *Life Is about Choices*, I

hope to share with you the opportunity to know your life's purpose and to change the course of your life. Identifying your core beliefs and values can transform your life in a very decisive way. I invite you to create your intentional reality and to live your best life possible.

A Peek Behind The Curtain

There is an ever-increasing number of people searching for more meaning and purpose in their lives. Tired of being just casual observers, many are now seeking answers to the many questions in their unfulfilled lives. We are fortunate to live in an age of increasingly improved technology, sophisticated sciences, and nearly unlimited informational resources. It is important to realize that the necessary information and resources are available to those seeking answers. In this country, many individuals and entire families have abandoned their traditional churches because of church politics or sexual abuse of children by the clergy. Many of these people have adopted the cafeteria-style selection of a church that suits their particular beliefs. Even more have left traditional church memberships, because they have not found definitive or profound answers to substantiate their intuitive and core beliefs.

Our universe is in constant evolution and so it is with the human condition. For many years until now, people around this earth have observed a remarkable and growing spiritual awakening. There are now numerous books and other materials available regarding an intention-driven life, living deliberately with purpose, and many other approaches to personal and spiritual growth. There is also evidence of a changing spiritual axis of the earth. Many of the centuries-old spiritual traditions and beliefs of East Asia and India are now being embraced by people in a light of spiritual awakening in the United States. At the same time, many developing Asian and middle-eastern countries are exchanging their centuries-old beliefs to embrace a capitalistic or monetary creed. The entire planet is also experiencing a larger spiritual renaissance. These are exciting times, and we are at an evolutionary milestone.

In 1943, noted psychologist Abraham Maslow developed his theory of human needs and motivation. He described the theory as resembling a pyramid with five ascending levels. The larger, base level was that of the basic, essential needs of food, shelter, and physical comfort. The second level was that of physical and psychological safety, and security. A third, smaller level, included the need for love and relationships. Higher still, the fourth level listed respect, self-esteem, and prestige with recognition from others. The pinnacle, or highest level of the pyramid, describes the human need of self-fulfillment and self-actualization—to realize one's full potential. Perhaps it's time to maximize our awareness and knowledge of ourselves beyond the Maslow theory basics of comfort and physical needs. Self-realization or fulfillment will likely include finding our true identity in a spiritual awakening.

A spiritual awakening is best described as finding our true inner being, or consciousness, not as an intellectual exercise, but as a self-actualization—a return to the source of our being. When we learn to separate our true inner being from that of identifying our being as the thinking mind, we may then answer the call to love and beauty. Unfortunately, not everyone can, or will, find an awakening.

In Matthew 22:14 it is noted, "Many are called, but few are chosen."[1] A smaller number of people are never called. There are, of course, those people not the least bit interested in spirituality. Others will seek an awakening but never find it. There are many more people seeking an enlightenment, believing it to be enlightenment of the mind, to find the ultimate wisdom and purpose of our lives. The personal, spiritual awakening that I describe is much more than the wisdom of a gathered knowledge. An accumulated knowledge is nothing more than dead matter, useless data, unless it is used to better the lives of others. *A spiritual awakening is the realization of our inner spiritual being, separated from any identification with the ego-based identification with the mind.*

There is also a spiritual awakening occurring within our global population. As more and more people come to the spiritual awakening, so our planetary society evolves. Because of the choices that we have made, our paths are many and varied. Some of us have included study and learning—looking for something that would answer our many questions. Sometimes we begin our search by looking at Eastern philosophy or theology, perhaps reinforced with a study of metaphysics and the sciences. Knowledge is a great thing, particularly when shared for the benefit of others, but a spiritual awakening does not depend upon an expanded knowledge. In recent years, we have witnessed a substantial increase in the number of resources that focus directly upon the spiritual longing of the many people searching for answers. Much like everything else in our instant-societies, many people want it now—instant answers, knowledge and enlightenment. Enlightenment comes to us in bits and pieces of sudden awareness of matters that we previously did not fully understand. The knowledge and answers that we seek may be found within the human body temple as the entirety of creation is within each of us. We need only to make the decision and to look within.

When we decide that we wish to find meaning and purpose, and decide to change our lives, the process can be very simple. We need to examine our core beliefs and values. Our core values and beliefs are truly our biology and our destiny. *It is important to realize that our dominant thoughts and beliefs create our reality.*[2] What we have thought about and believed in the past has created our reality today, and what we believe today will determine our future. We need not be destined to repeat our mistakes, our suffering, or to slow our evolutionary progress. We have a choice. We do not need to wait for repeated, unwanted experiences to be brought to our awareness when we can, instead, prompt new and rewarding life experiences.

Our beliefs have developed over time and were influenced by our parents, our friends, teachers, and many other individuals, and also the events in our lives. Our beliefs have become a filter through which we perceive our present reality and create our future. Our beliefs also define how we see ourselves and recognize our capabilities. It is important that we realize that a single belief represents but one of many possibilities. When we begin to see the many possibilities available, we can then change our beliefs, our perception, and our experiences. To change our experience is to create our own unique reality. Many of our choices and actions are based upon our unconscious retention of our prior experiences and habits that we have formed. If we bring these habits and beliefs into our conscious awareness for examination, we can then transform our entire belief-filtering system and direct our biology and our destiny. Our beliefs reverberate with an energy field that also affects both our feelings and physical health. When we embrace the higher vibratory energies of positive thoughts and beliefs, our bodies perceive them and respond in positive ways.

In my previous book, *Wisdom of the Heart: Create Your Own Reality*, I suggested that we must examine our beliefs and values and then decide what it is that is most important to us as matters of the heart, and then create our desired reality. This continues to be true. However, there is an important issue that I did not describe adequately enough in that previous writing. And that is: *our human awareness is consciousness without thought.* Our personal growth and awakening depends solely upon our coming to an awareness of our true inner being; thereafter, we do not have to think about it. Our daily choices come to us as coincidences, and our human intuition provides us with correct choices.

Many people have come to the belief that we have little or no choice or free will— that our volition is only a false definition of part of our mental functioning. It has also been said that everything in our human existence has been predetermined and therefore we have no free will, or choice. The truth of the matter is that every aspect of our lives has been predetermined at a higher level of consciousness and creation. It is because of our existence and our awareness in the lower physical–emotional realm that we appear to have the capability of free will and decisions. So, while we are operating in this physical world, we can use our own volition or free will and change our lives. This too was predetermined! Whatever your belief is, believe that even a predetermined role for your life might also include the coincidental opportunity to gain the knowledge and the capacity to change your beliefs, your present lifestyle, and your future.

In the seventeenth century, the French philosopher Rene Descartes altered history when he developed a theory that earned him the title "The Father of Modern Philosophy." Descartes declared, "I think, therefore I am." Rene Descartes was a brilliant philosopher, lawyer, and scientist. However, he either failed to recognize our innate, spiritual essence of consciousness or he ignored this element of our being. Descartes was not aware of his awareness—he had not yet awakened. Over the past four centuries, we have sufficiently evolved to better know and understand the difference between our mental capacity and that of our core spiritual being. Many people now believe that Descartes has retarded our progress in philosophy as well as our understanding of humanity. We should take a closer look and examine the elements of human consciousness. Both objective and subjective reality also need to be examined. What makes matters even more interesting is the phenomena of synchronicity as it relates to manifest reality.

Our world changes dramatically when we suddenly discover how synchronicity works, and we realize the interconnectedness of all things and events. In the 1939 Warner Brothers movie, *The Wizard of Oz*, Dorothy and friends looked behind the curtain and found not only the wizard, but also a new reality. Would you like to peek behind that curtain and see for yourself?

Human Awareness and Consciousness

Because our human awareness is essential in changing our core beliefs, we should take a closer look at the elements of our consciousness. The basic elements of our human consciousness are attention, awareness, perception, cognition, imagination, and memory. Attention is the probe of our awareness. For example, your attention at this moment is directed to these words before you, yet you are simultaneously aware of the voice in your head and of the fact that you are reading.

External sights, sounds, scents, and other things can also attract and hold your attention without your intention to have them do so. Our attention feeds millions of bits of information per second into our cognitive awareness.

Perception allows us to recognize only a small portion of the information received, and our minds automatically filter this information. The human mind will subjectively compare any new data with that of our past experiential knowledge. Each of us has probably met another person considered to be narrow-minded, refusing to see or accept anything new or challenging. If we have conditioned our minds and see things with an open mind, we will tend to be more accepting of new information. It is quite natural for the human mind to become analytical, using both inductive and deductive reasoning. We may then examine and question the validity of the information and seek even more data. There is an interesting relationship that develops between our capacity for perception and the development of our beliefs and values. As our human perception grows by experience, we form a personal belief system. Both our perception and our beliefs are flexible and changing. Over time, and with sufficient experience, our beliefs become a filter for our perception of information and events. Conversely, our perception can also influence and reform our beliefs.

Of all the elements of consciousness, human awareness is the most important. Awareness is that part of our consciousness that connects us to a creative universal intelligence. *Human awareness is consciousness without thought.* Actually, there are two aspects of our human awareness. It is our cognitive awareness that allows us to be cognizant, or mindful, of our immediate thoughts and the sensations received through our five senses. All creatures have various, evolved levels of awareness, but only we humans have evolved to the extent that we are aware of our awareness. For example, an insect has a basic awareness that allows it to recognize fire as a threat. Other life-forms are aware of threats to their survival depending upon their level of evolution. The second aspect of human awareness is that of our larger spiritual awareness: consciousness without thought. When Moses had asked God of His name, the response was reported to have been, "I am that I am."[3] An example of both aspects of our awareness is that which we call our conscience. Remember those times when you had done something and immediately knew or felt that it was wrong? Our innate consciousness knows the truth and brings it forward to our cognitive, or mindful, awareness. Our entire life is about choices, decisions, and consequences based upon our subjective beliefs and values.

Both aspects of our awareness can be enlarged or expanded. For example, we can use the mind to study in a learned manner and become a scholar, yet we might not grow in spiritual awareness. Our cognitive human awareness gathers knowledge from our experiences and stores the knowledge in both our conscious and our subconscious mind. Our capacity for memory also allows us to be aware of past experiences that may influence not only our future choices, but also the creation of our new life experiences.

Once we find our true inner being, changes will manifest not only in our attitudes and thought processes, but also in our spiritual awareness. A spiritual awareness is our guide in making many choices. Needless to say, when we awaken spiritually, our lives will change in profound ways.

Many of us have experienced an out-of-body consciousness during heart surgery or other life-threatening events. When we travel out of the human body and observe other physical activity, it becomes very apparent that our consciousness is a silent, formless energy of pure awareness. This experience is one of our awareness—devoid of thought and words.

> Take a flight of fancy. Come, fly with me for a moment. Close your eyes and imagine seeing yourself out of doors, sitting comfortably in a lawn chair. Notice the clothing that you are wearing, and notice, too, your view from overhead. Now imagine yourself floating twenty feet above your own body, still seated below in the lawn chair. This experience is known as an out-of-body, or astral, experience. Next,

imagine seeing yourself in the lawn chair as you float effortlessly above at five hundred or even five thousand feet in altitude. Long-distance travel is also available via your imagination, and it requires no words for recognition. Who is it that is silently flying? As a licensed helicopter and fixed-wing pilot, I can attest to the joy of all methods of flight.

Is this experience, then, one of a subjective or objective reality? For those of us who further believe that there is another realm of existence beyond our physical death, we also expect that our spiritual awareness or consciousness does not die, but continues on to another dimension. This experience will depend upon our level of awareness. If we believe in a realm called hell, then it will be exactly as we have thought it to be. If we create another reality that was formed by more favorable beliefs, then it will also be much as we believed it to be.

The human capacity for imagination is obviously another important link, or element, in creating our beliefs and our future. As we think and believe, so we shall become. The people remembered throughout history as being successful have had vision; they have used their imaginations for great accomplishments. The very least that we can do for ourselves is to imagine a happy and meaningful life. *Where attention goes, energy flows.* Once we are aware that our beliefs and our dominant thoughts determine our future, we can take the responsibility and the opportunity to develop positive, meaningful life experiences. A meaningful life with purpose will include positive values behind our choices, decisions, and our actions. Our life's choices should be based upon honesty, compassion, trust, humility, kindness, sincerity, and many other basic aspects. Consider for a moment, those persons we have witnessed who were making choices based upon a self-centered greed, malice, and dishonesty. What could these people possibly see as their core values and their basic purpose in life?

The whole of our human consciousness includes the larger area of sub-consciousness that is more often described as our super-consciousness. Our super-consciousness controls and maintains our body's autonomic systems in ways that we do not yet fully understand. An even larger, unexplored region of the super-consciousness suggests that we have an undeveloped potential or capability for a future use.

Psychology defines consciousness as our capacity for thought, cognition, volition or will power, emotion, and sensation. The combination of these elements allows us to change or expand our conscious awareness. At any given moment of our lives, our conscious awareness is in a *state-of-being*. Even while sleeping, we enter an altered state-of-being and can experience various events, emotions, and other sensations. All of our experiences in the physical body and our experiences of the mind and beyond are experienced as temporary states-of-being in conscious awareness. In a conscious awareness, our mental state-of-being is not necessarily dependent upon those things brought to our perception. In an objective reality, emotional and physical influences can bring us to changing states-of-being. When we identify ourselves with the ego-mind, we then expose ourselves to the random, ever-changing influences of others and of events occurring about us. Our ego-mind demands more and more to support its own identity. That which we believe about our present existence will cause things to be just as we expect. We are then experiencing a state-of-mind as opposed to a calm, centered, state-of-being.

There are several levels of human consciousness, and each of us function at one or more of these levels simultaneously. The various levels of consciousness are not stratified with exact boundaries separating each level, but instead, overlap to varying degrees. The first level, of course, is that of the gross physical plane of our existence. The next, or second, level is the astral plane. Even higher, the next level, or causal plane, is often referred to as the universal mind. Meditation techniques can reveal even higher realms of human consciousness, but there are no words to adequately describe the unique, personal experiences found in this manner.

Many people believe that our consciousness is *just there* and that we cannot change our consciousness. Others know that we can alter or raise our own consciousness with an increased awareness. If we are simply coasting though life without control, our consciousness will create and influence our life experiences. Our past experiences, stored in consciousness, will be retrieved to create even more of the same old kinds of random, unwanted experiences. It is obvious, too, that our unwanted past experiences also affect our life's choices, decisions, and actions. It becomes important to know and understand these human capacities as we create our individual realities, and to invite the experiences that we desire. We have the capacity of the mind, with awareness, to step outside of our consciousness, look at consciousness, and realize what has been happening in our lives.

There are basically two ways by which we can begin to change our lives, and both methods involve the law of attraction to obtain optimal results. We can, first, acknowledge the necessity and the usefulness of the ego-mind in planning and doing things in accordance with the laws of the natural universe. Then, with the use of our ego-mind, our will power and imagination, we can learn to merge with the creative force of the universe to manifest material and mental change for improving our physical surroundings. This is the basis of intentional living. It may sound good, but this is still our mind running our lives. Many people have been successful in their endeavors using their minds to determine their reality and their purpose in life. Mentally deciding upon a purpose in life, however, will not provide a sustainable future. Our existence and future in this external life are fleeting and subject to change. Understand that there is a critical difference between *doing* things to fulfill an intentional, mindful purpose and that of the primary purpose of our *being*. The practice of thinking and doing things to fulfill an ever-changing life purpose is chaotic and leads only to continued frustration and suffering. Can we really believe then that we should depend upon our thinking capability? Just imagine, for a moment, that our brains are wired to a loudspeaker with our thoughts broadcast publicly. In that case we can easily understand why others might cross the street to avoid us. Unrecognized and uncontrolled, the human mind and ego is defensive and rationalizes input to justify everything to fit our needs. The ego will eventually take control of our decided life purpose and corrupt or destroy it. The human ego loves the idea of having a systematic mental approach to obtaining spiritual growth. Our capacity to analyze systems and concepts can only present an intellectual prize to us. Our perceived esteemed levels of intellectual sophistication and knowledge may actually be a hindrance to quieting the mind and finding the inner, silent listener.

A preferred, second, method of changing our lives, is that of living in the flow of the creative force of the universe. Some will call this living in the will of God, the Tao, or Allah. More of a spiritual quest, this method centers our attention upon our awareness and our consciousness. Consider that *our true being, a perfect consciousness, is far more beautiful than anything that we could wish to become.* Our human awareness is not the same as our capacity for thinking. Awareness is our connection or presence within the universal intelligence and our awareness is consciousness without thought. Just sit quietly in your awareness and be the silent listener. Some call this, "being in the now." Listen to the incessant chatter of the ego-mind running uncontrolled. It is the mind and ego that shouts, "I am this and that." Or "I have this or that." The human ego worries about the reputation and might cause you to ask, "What then, of my reputation?" The answer is, "What others think of you is their business." More importantly, others may know you better than you know yourself. Sit quietly, go within to find the silent listener and come to better know yourself. When we go within and find our true being, we then learn to be confident in that knowledge. A quiet self-confidence need never be boastful or fearful. Listen to your ego, your thoughts, and see that the majority of them are random and wasteful. The mind is a powerful and useful tool for accomplishing many constructive things, and we should use it as a tool to function in the physical world. However, when we know the difference between thinking, doing, and that of being, we cease to identify ourselves with the ego-mind, our reputation, and our physical and material attachments. The thinking mind then becomes subservient to awareness, and we can align our emotions and thoughts with our true identity. Using the mind as a tool then allows our thoughts and attitudes to become the keys to attracting a new reality. Our thought processes become words and our words, reinforced with attitude, become actions and habits. Any life worth living with purpose and meaning requires that we align our thoughts, our words, and our actions with our intended objectives or goals.

When we look to our true being or spiritual essence and find our true, primary purpose, our physical and mental existence will automatically evolve or change for the better. The very functions of our being, or consciousness, are that of love, beauty, peace, and joy. Only when we experience this state of being, in awareness, do we find a meaningful purpose in accordance with the natural flow of a perfect universe. It is at this point that our choices are shown to us via coincidence, or synchronicity, and it becomes so very easy to make the right choice and to do the right thing.

Our elegant universe contains everything we need to know in order to acquire peace, joy, love, beauty, health, wealth, knowledge, and spiritual awakening. There are many unseen, not yet fully understood forces and powers in our universe that can enable us to raise our awareness and consciousness to our full potential. How we define for ourselves our purpose in life will also define how we begin to use the creative powers available.

There is a magical way in which the intelligence and the creative force in our universe respond to our requests for life-altering change. This creative force has been described as the heavenly, ethereal substance of our universe, and many religious traditions have called the phenomena the work of God—the Holy Ghost. John 1:1, notes, "In the beginning was the Word, and the Word was with God, and the Word was God."[4] Both the ancient Greek philosopher and scientist Socrates, and his student, Plato, referred to the universal ether as the aether, and called it the fifth element, in addition to earth, air, fire, and water. Even today, the fifth element is believed by some to be that which connects our thoughts to a universal consciousness.

Historically, religious scripture, text, and policies have made reference to a secret knowledge, but many of these have been changed and rewritten. These scriptures and text have been passed along to the faithful only after being subjected to interpretation by religious leaders. Many original scriptures and texts available still contain words, phrases, and references written in an esoteric manner and remain unknown to the average reader. In India, the Sikh tradition refers to the Word as Shabd, or Sound Current. Science has identified the plasma as an electromagnetic field that permeates the entire universe. Recent writings have referred to this creative force as The Secret. It is actually the secret knowledge of the ancients that is also known as the law of attraction.

The Law of Attraction

The science of physics proposes that everything in our physical universe consists of vibratory energy. Light, sound, solids, liquids, body tissue—all things—are comprised of energy, which science can now measure. We are energy beings in an energized universe. Science has further demonstrated that energy is often transferred or changed, but never lost. Medical science has shown that our cells have both a basic intelligence and a memory. All of our body cells communicate with one another to function. Consider that our cellular bodies are listening to our minds through our thoughts. Nowadays the medical community is only awakening to a new realm of research in the causation and treatment of our biology. The biology of the human body includes more than fifty billion cells, and the energy of human thought has the greatest influence upon our cells. The unseen energy produced by our thoughts is very powerful and is not without consequence. Within our universe of energy, our total being seeks balance, or homeostasis. Our evolving universe has purpose, and so it is for us as inhabitants. The laws of our universe are immutable and, therefore, predictable for our existence and use. Persons who work with healing energies and human body energy can attest to the power of these energies.

Vibratory electromagnetic forces hold electrons and protons together, and atoms combine to form molecules. In the atomic field of electromagnetic energies, opposites attract. Even our bodies are comprised of electrically charged particles in balance with the opposing electromagnetic earth fields. Our thoughts, however, become energy forms at a subatomic level. The studies of theoretical physics and quantum mechanics have explored the sublevel of energies in electromagnetic and superstring theories. At this level, energies do not attract opposites but, instead, attract the same and similar energies.

Our thoughts leave our minds as energy forms whether they are positive, negative, or neutral. Thought energy can be directed and received, as evidenced in the animal world with instinctual telepathy. For example, recall the belief that animals can instinctively sense fear in humans. These energies, too, are never lost. When we think negative thoughts, this energy will not only return to us, but also it will attract more of the same or similar energy to us. We have been attracting our life events with our thought energies. Positive thoughts cause positive energies to be drawn to us. Knowing this, we can change our lives and create positive, rewarding experiences in accordance with a primary purpose in life. Many people will call this living in the will of God, while others will call this living in the flow of the creative universal energy. For centuries, the law of attraction has been referred to in esoteric writings and ancient manuscripts, but the scientific community has not yet been able to provide explanations for the phenomena with quantum physics. Many scientists are critical of the law of attraction because they believe that if something cannot be documented, repeated, and measured, it cannot therefore exist.

The law of attraction states that like-attracts-like and that our thoughts attract and manifest our experience just as we have thought about it. Our dominant thoughts and beliefs will find a way to manifest in our reality. Our beliefs, desires, expectations, and even our earnest gratitude hold an immense power. Consider that we have both feelings and thoughts. Typically, our emotional feelings are the stronger of the two. When our thoughts are both positive and in alignment with our feelings, they provide a strong focus for action. This is an important issue when we consider the use of the law of attraction. In addition to our thoughts and feelings, our words and actions become even more powerful when aligned with our objectives. When our objective is to acquire something, we must focus on having it rather than on wanting it. If we continue to want something, we will be provided more opportunity to further want without having acquired anything. The universe cannot say, "No."

That which we think about and desire most will be given to us.

The law of attraction has often been referred to as the law of cause and effect. An old Chinese proverb reads, "Life is like an echo, what you send out will return to you." In the biblical sense, it is said, "As you sow, so shall you reap." Realize that our physical world, or reality, is not the cause, but the effect. We cannot manipulate the effect, but we can change the cause and create the effect. Creating our reality is that simple. One more thing—do not succumb to the age-old belief that we have to earn it to enjoy it. We do not have to earn anything—everything is readily available just for the asking. In the New American Standard Bible, according to the Gospel of Mark 11:24, Jesus was quoted as saying, "Therefore I say unto you, all things whatsoever ye pray and ask for, believe that ye shall receive them, and you shall have them." Let our thoughts be our prayer.

Laws are generally promulgated for compliance. If we decide to live by the law of attraction, then we must also obey the same law. When we decide to live with the law of attraction, we employ very simple but exact principles. The precise law of attraction requires the following:

1. DESIRE: Think enthusiastically about what it is that you want. Prioritize your values, and be careful what it is you ask for. Keep all of your thoughts, feelings, and visualizations positive and enthusiastic in nature. Your thoughts must match your feelings. The feelings of happiness and joy are very powerful and intensify your energies.

2. DECIDE: Know and decide, very specifically, what it is that you wish

for. Include your ownership and responsibility for the result.

3. ASK: Ask very specifically for what it is that you want. Include a reasonable time frame and specific amounts of tangible items. Your request may be vocalized, but it is your dominant thoughts that will manifest the change.

4. BELIEVE: Believe, as a matter of law, that your request will be manifest because you are a living part of the universal flow. God and the universe want you to be happy, and you owe it to yourself.

5. WORK: Work the request in your mind daily, in a positive manner. Imagine and visualize your request as manifest. Post in a convenient place, photos, drawings, or other graphic depictions of any physical items sought to remind you of the request.

You can also imagine item(s) in your hand, your home, your garage, or other location.

6. SHOW GRATITUDE: Think and say, "Thank you, God," or "Thank you, universe." Think it, say it, and genuinely feel the gratitude for the response to your request. With time, you can also say thanks for being reintegrated into the universal flow of things. Sincere gratitude is a very powerful energy and magnifies your intent.

When using the law of attraction, we cannot ask for something not to occur or ask for anything that would be injurious to others. For example, we cannot ask for a better life, as this implies the negative element that says we presently have an undesirable or unwanted life. The negative aspect of this position will only attract more of the same to our lives. We can begin by realizing that we already have a good life, are grateful for this, and that we simply wish to make changes to our lives.

Secondly, our request for something must be reasonable, and we must believe with total faith that it will happen as a matter of absolute law (cause and effect). We may request something to occur within a specified and reasonable time frame, but we will not know the exact timing of the occurrence for our request any more than we can possibly know of the many intricate, interwoven coincidences required to make it happen. We should not even think about how it will occur, as any doubt arising will negate the request. Many people believe that using the law of attraction is an integral part of their subjective reality.

The concept of a subjective reality holds that a belief system is one in which there is only one consciousness and you are that consciousness. You are the center of the universe. Anything and everything in your reality are simply projections of your thoughts. Consider for a moment that when you are asleep and dreaming, you create all of the people and circumstances of your dream and you can do whatever you wish in the context of the dream. It is a combination of your beliefs, imagination, and your intentions that creates the dream. The same is true when you awaken from the dream—your thoughts continue to create your reality. Knowing this, you can take control and change your destiny. Yes, you can make your dreams come true.

The description of objective reality supposes that all events and objects in creation are already existent and that we all see them in the same way. For example, there is a tree at location X, whether or not we see it or hear it. We will all see the same tree if we were to visit location X. In a subjective reality, the tree does not exist until we create it in our mind. Objective reality is independent of the mind, whereas subjective reality is dependent upon the mind for existence. Perhaps we enjoy both objective and subjective elements in our perceived reality. When a baby is born, the infant is not likely aware of his or her awareness and will experience an objective reality. Imagine that we go through life with a perception of objective reality, knowingly or otherwise. It is when we become aware of the difference that we can then use the law of attraction to create and experience in a subjective reality. Do you know what has been your experience of reality?

In the King James Bible, John 16: 24 reads, "Hitherto have you asked nothing in my name; ask and you shall receive, that your joy may be full." We routinely use the law of attraction to acquire our experiences, whether knowingly or otherwise. Have you ever asked for an open parking space in a crowded parking lot, only to have it occur immediately? Recall the times that you have thought about a distant friend only to have that friend suddenly phone or write to you. I will bet that many of us have, at some time or another, said, "God, get me through this and I will never do it again." And we once again got through the crisis.

When I first decided to test the law of attraction, I visualized a large amount of silver coins and bullion resting on the floor in my basement. I then joyously requested that the same silver come to my home. Within a two week time period, a friend brought his silver savings to my basement, asking that it be stored there temporarily. This was amazing! I had forgotten, however, to be specific in asking that the silver be mine.

Many years ago, I once stepped up to the tee with my golf club and announced to the others in my foursome that I was about to shoot a 185-yard, hole in one. At this age in my life, I could only occasionally break one hundred on a par seventy-two golf course. This day, I was a confident, amateur seventeen-year old. I teed the ball and began my swing. The moment I hit the ball with my club, I knew that the golf ball was headed for the hole on the distant green. With that one shot, I became the most talked about pro for the next week.

There is a distinct difference between making a wish hoping that it might occur and that of requesting an action with the faith and conviction that it will occur with certainty. When our faith is strong and we firmly believe in the law of attraction, our requests are answered quickly. When we request something, we cannot for a moment, ever, try to begin to understand just how it will happen. There may be hundreds of coincidental factors occurring behind the scenes, and our questioning can only cause doubt. With faith there is no doubt. Continued faith causes doubt to be replaced by an emotional enthusiasm. At this point, our thoughts coalesce with our feelings in a very powerful way. The more often our requests are answered, the stronger our faith then becomes—it is reciprocal.

For those persons further interested in a scientific approach, there is another method to increasing our awareness and our understanding of how our choices in life are made. A quick study of physics can show how our choices and decisions in life are truly dependent upon that same human awareness and knowledge. Using a computer with access to the Internet, type in the search item "space-time dimensions." We find the theories for many dimensions of our universe and our human existence. The basic four dimensions of objects in our reality include a point of existence, or origin, extending as a line to acquire a dimension of length. A second dimension is that of width, a third dimension is height, and a fourth dimension is time. For many years this was thought to be the acceptable four-dimensional description of our space-time continuum. More recently, some physicists have theorized that there are even more dimensions to our reality. The same physicists believe that each of the first three physical, spatial dimensions may also be expanded, each in their own time dimensions, resulting in at least six dimensions. Every moment in time contains the possibilities of multiple events or choices. It is believed by some that because of an unlimited number of dimensions available, it is the human observer that determines, or chooses, one of multiple choices available solely because of the observer's beliefs or awareness. There are other interesting phenomena involved with thought energies and manifesting our reality. One example has shown that the fifth classical element of the ether has a time delay. When we make repeated visualizations and requests for something, it is very much like the repeated strikes of a hammer upon a solid object. The request is accelerated proportionately.

We create not only our physical reality, but also we create events or occurrences in our lives. The theory of multiple, or parallel, universes is also very popular. Some physicists and others like me believe, further, that the choices we make will commingle, or integrate, with those choices made by others. Physicists have added the element of human experience to their theories in order to validate and complete the space-time reality. I have substituted the word awareness for the former term experience. Simply stated, we create our own reality, and we do so with our awareness, thoughts, and volition, or choices.

When brought to a point of making decisions, we should learn to depend upon our intuition for guidance. All too often the human mind and ego brings us to the lesser choice. Intuition is a very subtle knowing that comes to us as a "gut feeling" or "something we just knew intuitively." When synchronicity or coincidence brings us to a fork in the road, we learn to follow our intuition rather than the unreliable reasoning of the mind. We should go with the universal flow. Our human intuition is often misunderstood. Human intuition comes from the subconscious level of our mind to our cognitive awareness. Our intuition cannot be developed: it is simply there. We can, however, learn to recognize the intuitive thoughts brought to our awareness and develop our responses or choices accordingly. Our intuition will then increase in accordance with continued use. It is the rational, thinking analysis of the human mind that will alter, destroy, or recognize a bit of information that you intuitively know to be true without having previously thought about it. When we are presented with a coincidence or a series of coincidences, it is our intuition that first brings our awareness into focus. Incredibly, after we recognize the synchronicity of events, more coincidence will follow when we learn to trust and follow these unscheduled or unexpected events. When these events require a decision or a choice to be made, we can trust our human intuition to make the right choice every time.

It is when we consciously seek or request

something in changing our life that it becomes important in choosing between the gratification of a desire for physical, material acquisitions or that of acquiring spiritual growth and enlightenment. With knowledge of our true identity and a new state of being, our innate wisdom will lead us to surrender to the flow of our universe and love's call.

SWEET SURRENDER

When we come to realize and accept our being in consciousness as our true identity, we subjugate the human ego to a lesser role. For many years, this has been called a "sweet surrender." It reflects our humility in accepting the beckoning call of the universe to experience love and beauty. Some call this the surrender to the will of the Creator, God, the Tao, or Allah. For many others, it is simply living in the flow of the creative universe. In either case, one does not have to be of a religious persuasion.

Earlier, I mentioned the functions of the

soul as those of love, beauty, peace, and joy. The truth is that peace and joy follow quite naturally after we realize that love and beauty are the essence of our being. *The sweet surrender to love and beauty will forever change our beliefs, our perception, and therefore, change our lives.* The ego will resist the idea of surrender, but it can be done. The human ego causes doubt and reservations, and the very idea of any surrender may bring thoughts or fears of vulnerability. Giving so much of one's self can create in us a feeling of risk—the risk of being hurt or the fear of losing something. Actually, the sweet surrender to love will not cause us to lose our identity or our soul, but we will instead, find it. The ego is rooted in fear and competition, and fear is the opposite of love.

In a previous chapter on human awareness and consciousness, I mentioned the possibility of the human intellect and will power as being an obstacle to finding our inner being. Some people are even proud of their strong sense of will power and higher level of intelligence to the point of being stubborn. However, our volition and intellect are both elements of the mind, and the mind gives voice to our ego.

Consider that even the earliest forms of human life on earth were intelligent enough to know that there existed a creative force greater than themselves. Throughout history, people have feared and worshipped various gods and spirits without the benefit of the intellectual gains that we know today. Intellect and volition, however, can be useful in acquiring more knowledge of our biology and spiritual pursuits and the will power employed to provide determination in reaching our goals.

Once we know the difference between the ego-based mind and that of our true inner being, we can ask for help from the creative forces at work. The law of attraction will provide a remarkable response to our sincere requests. Life's choices will become remarkably easy decisions.

One of the easiest ways to subjugate the ego-mind is through the choice to experience prayerful gratitude and devotion. Prayer is the thoughts or words we use in voicing an earnest and humble plea or request to the creator. When we occupy our mind with humility and an earnest request or thank you, we instantly acknowledge a greater creative force. For centuries people have memorized scripted litanies and have called these words prayer. These prayers have served a purpose in their religious beliefs, but often these prayers become nothing more than a commitment to memory and ritual. By contrast, consider the simple but earnest words of thanks that are spoken from the heart rather than from the head.

The simplest of prayers need not resemble a chant or a mantra, and might be offered at any time of any day. For example, we can greet the dawn with sincere and joyful thanks as we anticipate another beautiful day. With practice and proper orientation, our meditation can extend to include all of our daily activities. This is actually a prayer that summons the law of attraction and all of the wondrous things it can bring to us. Try it and change your life! *When we embrace the idea that love is our core essence and central to our beliefs, we can begin to see beauty in all things.* Peace and joy will follow in abundance.

Meditation and introspection are the fastest methods of finding and experiencing the difference between the ego-based mind and our true being. Meditation has also been shown to have therapeutic benefits for both mind and body. It can actually change the brain serotonin, hormones, and other bodily functions in a positive way. Meditative techniques may vary from a rigid, ritualistic form to a relaxed, contemplative method. When we channel or concentrate our thoughts in a very powerful way of prayerful gratitude, we can subdue or control the ego with humility. This relaxed type of meditation is often called mindfulness meditation. Our human mind is capable of at least nine separate and simultaneous channels of communication and must be controlled and directed. There are some who fear meditation, believing that they may lose their identity and lose control of their rational mind. In fact, quite the opposite is true. In meditation, we simply learn to control our thoughts and find our true essence or identity. Our benefits are manifest physically, intellectually, and spiritually. Thus, in meditation we separate our thinking mind from our spiritual being.

A key to meditation is to sit comfortably with our eyes closed in a quiet environment, devoid of distractions. It also helps to begin by listening to our bodies; listen to the sounds of our breathing, heartbeat, and other body functions. A second important key to meditation is becoming aware of our thoughts—listening to the endless chatter of our mind. At this point we must ask ourselves, "Who is it that is listening? Who is the silent listener aware of the voice of our ego-mind?" The silent listener is your consciousness or soul. Meditation is that simple! Once we have experienced the awareness of the difference between the chatter of our mind and that of the silent listener, we can revisit this experience often. Many people refer to this revisiting as becoming centered in the refuge of our awareness. With practice, we can remain centered in our awareness throughout our daily activities. This then becomes so habitual as to become a realization, or experience of consciousness without thought.

It makes sense that in order to be doing things with our lives, we should first begin to intimately know our self and what is important to us. We must also know the tools and resources we have available to us. Introspection or meditation can show us our true, silent being and may help us identify our priorities in this life. When we surrender to love, we will continue doing things, but what we are doing will then be consistent with the creative force of the universe. This is simply aligning our actions of thinking and doing with a purpose for being able to serve a higher creative force. For example, some may question whether writing this book was not an act of thinking and doing. Yes it was, but with the proper orientation in love, my writing becomes an act in accord with the creative universe. My thoughts and this writing were the result of using my mind to serve the purpose of my being. Every morning I say, "Thank you," to a faceless, nameless universal spirit, also called as the Creator. I then ask for a visible sign or coincidence to tell me what I can do to serve a higher purpose this day. Often, some new information or an entire book chapter will flood into my consciousness to be written.

The tenets, or the principles of Buddhism, have withstood the test of time and we can also learn from them. The Buddhist tradition follows four basic principles in discovering, identifying, and abandoning the ego in order to find spiritual enlightenment. The Buddhists believe that we must meet the ego head-on in order to control and direct it. Quiet meditation, or introspection, will separate the ego-mind from our true being.

The first aspect is that of loving-kindness. Learn to think lovingly of all others and of all things. We are all connected—in thought, in vibratory energy, and in spirit. Even if, at first, we cannot feel loving toward others, we can learn to show kindness to all, and love and understanding will follow. Learn to love all of our creation. In creating our reality we become co-creators.

The second aspect, or tenet, is that of joy. We should fully appreciate joy when we experience it and learn to find happiness in all things and at all times. It's not so easy when we are fearful, uncertain, or upset, but, with practice, we can eliminate fear and doubt and learn to be comfortable with unexpected surprises, fears, losses, and other unsettling emotions.

A third aspect is that of compassion. Compassion begins by empathizing with others when we truly care about their well-being. Compassion is a sympathetic consciousness for the suffering or plight of others—a true understanding and sharing of their pain and emotional distress.

Freedom, the fourth aspect, means a freedom of mind. Freedom of mind requires practice in being completely open and honest—first with our self, and then with others. Fearlessness is a part of freedom. Fear is the byproduct of our ego and is the root cause of hatred, prejudice, and other unwanted, defensive thoughts and practices. When love finds us, fear dissolves. The entire universe appears different when seen through the eyes of love.

There are numerous disciplines, religions, and other belief systems and organizations to suit almost any path that we wish to pursue to obtain spiritual guidance. Many of these disciplines have been originated, managed, and supported by persons believed to be messengers of truth.

The Messengers

The ancient Greek aphorism of "Know thyself" was attributed, by Plato, to the philosopher Socrates (469–399 BC) Socrates is considered to be the founder of Western philosophy with his study of humanity, government, ethics, mysticism, and much more. Socrates remands the individual to go within the self to be converse with the pure and to first know the self before we can know truth. Messengers of the ultimate truth may have had a historical role or may have been simply a contemporary, inspirational speaker or teacher. Throughout history there have been many messengers. Many of these individuals have been past- or present-day religious leaders. There have been many messengers of differing societal status, and even today, there are many messengers among us. In today's multimedia age there are messengers, each with a unique style and approach, to an audience seeking that particular type of message and delivery. The spiritual messengers and Masters have taught timeless spiritual truths in a variety of ways reflecting the environment and the period in which they live. All of the spiritual messengers, teachers and leaders have instructed and taught others within their own realm or circle of influence. Look closely and see that all of these messengers have put forth a common teaching or message for us. That basic message is to go within the self and abandon the ego-self to find our true spiritual essence.

The messengers of today and of the past have been called gurus, avatars, prophets, Lords, Masters, clergy, mystics, and many other titles. One such messenger was known as the Buddha. More correctly, his name at birth was Siddhartha Gautama. Buddha was born in 563 BC, in Kapilvastu, in the region now called Nepal. Buddha literally means the *enlightened one*. The Buddha, born into nobility as a prince, denounced his heritage and wealth in order to seek a spiritual cleansing. More than a simple philosophy, the Buddhist religion follows an elaborate discipline to explore the self, examine one's ego, and to abandon the ego-self to find enlightenment.

A well-known early messenger, John the Baptist, foretold the coming of a King among men known as the Christ. John the Baptist, later known as Saint John, was the last of the Old Testament prophets. .

Another messenger was Jesus of Nazareth

and his was a simple teaching of love and compassion. His teachings were recorded as gospels. Unfortunately, after many years, the teachings became shrouded in mystery with parables and interpretations that resembled riddles when they became the foundation for a religion. Consider the words, "The kingdom of heaven is within, for when thine eye be single, thy whole body shall be filled with light." How can an uninformed person begin to understand that this might be a reference to the meditation at the third-eye center of one's head? If asked, could you describe who or what is meant by the term, Holy Ghost? To fully understand what is meant in passages of the Christian Bible and other religious writings requires an elevated human awareness and, perhaps, a learned teacher.

The Indian Sikh tradition of Radha Soami recognizes the enlightened teacher or guru as a Master. This discipline, too, asks that the student, or seeker, go within the body-temple in meditation to silence the ego-mind and find spiritual enlightenment.

In the sixth century, a messenger known as the prophet Muhammad believed that the original teachings of Christianity had been radically changed to a polytheistic order to accommodate the growing Christian religion. The creation of the holy trinity within the Christian church was considered not to be part of the original teachings. The creation of the Islamic religion provided a return to a monotheistic religion and the correct interpretations for Muslims. The prophet Muhammad believed himself to be a reformer in calling Muslims back to the original revelations given first to Moses, then to Jesus, and, finally, to himself.

In the United States, Chief Joseph of the Nez Perce Indian tribe was a famous spiritual leader and medicine man.

Another Native American spiritual leader named Black Elk was considered one of the greatest spiritual leaders of twentieth-century North America.

Throughout the ages, there have been messengers, Masters and other teachers, sometimes called Saints. Historically, these messengers, Masters and spiritual teachers, have been both men and women graced with the spiritual truths. Examples of a few of the women are Sri Anandamayi Ma and Mirra Alfassa (The Mother). Another contemporary teacher was Sister Theresa. Many people believe her to be a Saint, and others, a spiritual Master. Still others believe that she was a spiritual leader and a teacher of love and compassion—living by example. She is exactly who you think she is. The commonly held belief is that there are two kinds of spiritual Masters. The first is that of a liberated person who has found spiritual realization through a dedicated life of study and devotion, wherein enlightenment and realization is an act of grace from God. The second is an individual who has also dedicated his or her life in search of spiritual truths and has found realization under the guidance of an existing spiritual Master.

Today, there are numerous knowledge-able and gifted messengers known to us as spiritual Masters, leaders, writers, and teachers. These gifted persons have attained higher levels of awareness, each different from the others, but all of them knowing that we have a life of choices. The higher their level or state of awareness, the more clearly defined their message. We then at-tach various names or titles depending upon our own beliefs or defined reality. We can now see why our human awareness is the most important aspect of our human consciousness.

Some of these extraordinary teachers

and writers have proven to be very inspirational with their message and life-changing knowledge. This new knowledge or awareness changes our beliefs, our values, and our life choices. These individuals have devoted their lives to serving as guides to those seeking a spiritual awakening and they have provided valuable knowledge and insight to many of us. We can learn from their shared wisdom without necessarily subscribing to any particular religion or organized discipline. Regardless of our present levels of awareness, we can always gain additional knowledge from these teachers and often reaffirm that which we have come to know and live.

When we wish to change our lives, it usually begins with a deep sense of yearning for something missing in our lives. In seeking to change our reality, we come to realize that there is a vast difference between our physical–emotional experience and that of our core spiritual being. It is only when we truly commit to change, that coincidence will provide the timely words or the introduction of that special person into our lives. When the seeker is ready, the Master appears. Many people have traveled thousands of miles to seek out a teacher, guru, or Master. Having located this teacher, these same people believe that it was by their own will and effort that they did so. If they were to look beyond their own ego at the coincidences, they would likely find that it was the teacher who had found the seeker. Most likely, it was the law of attraction answering their fervent wish for love and guidance. Our intuition and human awareness can help us in recognizing the importance of the workings of the many coincidences in our lives provided by the law of attraction. When we follow our intuition and coincidence, we instinctively know the truth when we see or hear it.

For anyone who considers his or her self to be a seeker of the truth, a word of caution is advised. Do not be too proud of the fact that you are considered to be a dedicated seeker. The seeker is often caught up in all of the knowledge discovered along the way while seeking, forgetting the original purpose of the search. Remember, that if you identify yourself as a seeker, you will most likely be a seeker forever after, and never be a finder.

The person that I describe as a messenger may well be the same person that others call a Master or prophet. What we make of these matters depends upon our level of awareness and understanding. Ask the messenger who he is, and the messenger will likely tell us, "I am who you think I am." This is true, as each of us create the details of our own reality with our beliefs. Unfortunately, we sometimes meet charismatic individuals and elevate them to an unrealistic status. They become exactly who and what we think they are. If we place these people upon a pedestal, these teachers or messengers will, in time, likely fall.

The messengers can provide guidance to others with personal instruction in meditation techniques and in developing acceptable lifestyles and life choices. These teachers or guides can also explain the secret knowledge contained in historical writings, teachings, and practices. Often, the seeker will be provided personal, historical, and scientific anecdotal examples to illustrate the path to an increased human awareness and consciousness. Historically, the gurus, Masters, or Bhagwans have advised their followers or spiritual seekers, to give up their minds, their bodies and their wealth in order to find spiritual wisdom. Because of their perception of the guru as a god-like deity, many people then bestow their monetary savings, vehicles, and property upon the teacher. They often offer their bodies for sexual favors to the Master and become cult-like followers. Their reality and perception comes into perfect alignment with the words of the teacher, "I am who you think I am." The original message was meant to suggest that our mind, our body, and any wealth that we have accumulated, was made possible only through the grace of our Creator. When we can separate our true being from our mental and physical worldly attachments, we can find truth. The messenger's primary role is that of bringing others to their full human potential and the realization of love and beauty as the ultimate truth of their existence.

Many of us began our search for spiritual growth believing that at some point in time, we could find an instant and complete enlightenment as though we had been tapped on the forehead with a magic wand. Many years later, our realization is that enlightenment comes unexpectedly, in small bits and pieces. The bits and pieces then begin to fall into place and we experience something called the *ah-hah* moment, when we suddenly come to know and understand something previously not known.

Whenever we meet a messenger and subscribe to his or her beliefs, we do not discard our individual responsibilities. Remember, the messenger is not responsible for our reality, our life, or our choices; we are.

BEAUTY AND THE BEHOLDER

Beauty is one of the core aspects of our true identity. An old saying goes, "Beauty is in the eye of the beholder." At first thought, beauty appears to come only from external sources for our recognition. Beauty, however, is already within each of us as a function of the soul, or consciousness, much like love and joy, and does not require thought. Remember, our consciousness includes a silent awareness or consciousness without thought. Human consciousness is not a part of, or a function of, the mind. Our awareness can bring thoughts to our mind, usually manifest as words, but our awareness of beauty requires no words. The beauty that we see or hear externally is simply a reflection of our inner self, brought to our cognitive awareness. Beauty is a choice that we can make; yes, beauty is a choice! We can choose to see beauty rather than ignore it. Remember, our attitudes and feelings affect our thoughts, and our thoughts, in turn, determine our future.

Beauty is thought to be obvious to us because of our capability to see and hear the pleasing harmony and patterns in nature. The language of nature is beauty and beauty provides joy. Each of us can remember watching a beautiful, glowing, red sunset or recall the song of a wren, singing its heart out to greet the dawn! Look further and we can visualize the silent strength in a majestic old oak tree! Look to autumn and we can picture every leaf become a flower. Our cognitive experience of beauty does not require any deductive or inductive analytical thought to recognize the joy in what we have seen or heard. To be one with nature is to simply exist quietly in the present moment and become part of the flow of the universe. These are timeless moments, rather than moments in time. Stop here and recall those timeless moments that you have experienced. Did they not involve beauty, peace, joy, or love? We can practice living in the present moment of awareness and bring about an incredible change in our lives. This is the choice that we can make.

Unfortunately, not everyone can, or will, come to the realization that love and beauty are the ultimate truth of our existence. Too many people today are seldom happy in their roles. Perhaps they have become victims of their own experience and continue to believe that they have been given a difficult, unchangeable lot in life.

For some, it is really difficult to see much beauty in our world. Even so, our world, our reality, can be a much more wondrous experience just with the choice of changing our perception to a positive one. In creating a change in our lives and beliefs, it behooves each of us to realize the importance of love and beauty—they are the essence of our true being. A good place to begin with is our recognition of the physical, mental, and spiritual beauty within each one of us in our human form. The human body is such a marvelous creation that retains the capability to produce anything and everything that we could possibly need.

The vast scope of nature is filled with turbulence, violence, death, and decay in a balanced act in the ever-changing theater of a visible and invisible universe. We must choose to look for and recognize the beauty that is not so obvious in this infinite and powerful world. We can learn to appreciate a world filled with the smallest, intricate, and most amazing life-forms. Our recognition of beauty should include a true love of all forms of creation with an understanding of the interconnectedness of all things. In the natural world, even the seemingly random acts of nature are actually in a perfect order and balance. We need only to look about us to see how our societies have interrupted and desecrated our natural world. Perhaps, it is time to begin to change our ways and to change many of our decisions.

In 1979, I was given a very expensive, commercial grade camera. I became familiar with the Minolta camera and used it to document community events and other activities. Within a few weeks, I could not resist my urges to begin photographing animals, birds, children, sunsets, and most anything else that appeared worthy of recording on film. Composition, balance, referencing, and other aspects of photography came easily to my inventory of skills. But after several months, a strange thing happened—I began to see beauty everywhere. While watching a flight of geese at sunset over a magnificent shore scene, I was left standing in awe. I had completely forgotten to film the fleeting scene. Now, a rose became more than just a pretty flower. Through the camera lens I discovered subtle but exquisite colors, textures, forms, and purpose of being, for both the rose and for myself. I felt as though the camera lens had functioned as a funnel to focus my attention and awareness, as I had been too busy with life's activities to stop and see the roses. Today, I continue to take photographs, much like those of a craftsman, knowing that I can never duplicate the natural beauty experienced. Mine is now a much deeper knowledge and sense of true beauty.

Whether we are looking at celestial bodies or a very small insect, the beauty and elegance of nature is far greater than the scope of man-made copies of beauty in art and science. The depictions in art that we revere as beautiful are only the work of a craftsman, reflecting the beauty that he or she sees. The art piece then evokes the same awareness of an inner beauty in the observer. When we choose to look for beauty everywhere, we find it not only in those things physical, but also in more subtle things like a silent smile, the laughter of children, the strength of the human spirit, and the marvel of synchronicity— coincidence.

Synchronicity, or coincidence, is provided by the continuous ebb and flow of our energy universe. The unexpected and unique events that we often experience and refer to as coincidence are the synchronicity of our universe. It is synchronicity that provides the manifestation and delivery of those things we have requested of the universe. Coincidence plays such an important role in our lives and yet many people do not understand the phenomena. Some will say that there is no such thing as coincidence as all events in our lives are preordained as necessary for the overall integration of our affairs. Nevertheless, these events must still coincide. Learn to see the beauty in the synchronicity and the exquisite timing of the many events interwoven into our lives. Once we can recognize the manner in which synchronicity prevails, we can then align our mentality and our daily activities to coincide with the universal flow of energy and events. In the 1960s, a popular expression was to, "Go with the flow." This saying holds true today as well.

Love's Call

Love is a function of the human soul and not of the mind. We do not decide or choose to experience love but we can, however, choose to enjoy love to the fullest when love visits us. Love is not a product of the mind and cannot be taught or learned. Over many centuries, numerous poets and philosophers have tried with difficulty, to describe love. They have described love using labels such as philos, eros, agape, unconditional, transcendental, and even a puppy love. Love then begins to appear as a mental function to be decided upon and abandoned at will. Because the human mind analyzes, dissects, and categorizes everything, it is inevitable that love has been described in so many ways. The human mind usually destroys a loving relationship when we develop expectations of others that are unfulfilled. Of course, over time, people change their values and their behaviors often causing an imbalance of expectations. All too often, people think that they are in love and realize too late that love was never part of their mental circus. Or, if it was love that they had experienced, their egos had destroyed it. This is in contrast to the love that is the essence of our spiritual being. We are love; love is the realization of the soul, much like beauty, joy, and truth. And our love is meant to be shared with others.

There is only one love, and it is a shared intimacy that determines the extent of our loving relationships with everyone and every thing. When we love two people, we do not love one person more than another. Love is love, and the difference between the two persons is the difference in the extent of intimacy shared with either person. Intimacy is shared not only with other people, but also at various levels with all of our creation. Take the time necessary to think about it for a moment. What is it that you enjoy in life at an intimate, personal level? It is your creation, your reality. Learn to see creation as intimately yours. Then explore and learn to love all of your creation as an awakened, realized person. There are neither any techniques, nor any mental process by which we can grant ourselves the acquisition of love, but love will find us when we choose to better know our true selves.

How many people do we know, who exist on a day-to-day basis, going from one crisis to another? It is as though their lives depended upon crisis for value or confirmation of worth. Many people become victims of their past experiences and find it difficult to let go of their natural ego instinct to become defensive or guarded. They often then choose a neutral position, fearing a further sense of loss or emotional injury. Past emotional experiences may have challenged their trust and loving spirit. When they experienced sorrow, pain, grief, or despair, it was actually love that formed the basis upon which these emotions were compared. We live in a world of opposites, with light and dark, good and bad, etc. To the extent that we can experience love, so too is the depth of our experience of sorrow and pain. If we choose a neutral state centered between love and loss, then there is nothing ventured and nothing gained or lost. Others will retreat to a position of hope. Many will only hope that things will occur or get better for them. Do they also hope that the Creator knows what he is doing? Hope only serves to remind us that hope is a mental affair. We can create our own reality with faith, knowledge, and awareness. That is our choice.

Sometimes our lessons come hard and are repeated until they are learned. We can choose a life with purpose and continue to live and feel vibrantly alive and fearless knowing that our indomitable inner being will survive no matter the conditions. We can learn to be confident and secure in our true identity and then be able to live with our sensitivity and to say with confidence that which we think and feel with others.

Many of the study materials available today have stated that there is no adequate description of human consciousness. I have to disagree and propose that our human consciousness is that of love. Consider that God is love, and conversely, love is God. Were we not made in the image of the

Creator? The image was certainly not of a physical body, but of the spirit—of love! In Genesis 1:27 it is noted, "God created man in His own image, in the image of God He created him; male and female He created them."[5] I truly believe that this is so. It is also my belief that in the past years, both of the words—God and love—have been over-used and misused to the extent that both words now require an explanation when used. I am a spiritual person but no longer a follower of any religion. The God that I know is very powerful and generous—the faceless, nameless Creator. We can better know God with our hearts than with our minds. It was Mahatma Gandhi who once stated, "Man can only describe God in his own poor language."

Having attended a Catholic elementary school as a young boy, I was told that God loved me and that I should fear the wrath of the Lord. This made very little sense to me until one spring day nearing the completion of the second grade. I was seven years old at the time and not considered a very good student. Even at this early age I saw little benefit in memorizing bible phrases that I did not fully understand. Our black-robed nuns were thought to be wardens rather than teachers. Sister Agnes had it in for me from the start of the year and she seemed to enjoy whacking me with a steel-edged ruler whenever I could not recall one of her rules. I could tell by her looks that she would need very little excuse to make a career of assaulting me. Sister Agnes wanted not only my mind, but also my body and soul.

On this particular day, an elderly priest visited our class and collected our catechisms, or books of scripture and prayer. He advised our class of thirty kids that he would present awards to those who maintained their books in good condition. Of course, mine was like brand new, having not been used very often. You can imagine the look on old Sister Agnes's face when my name was called to receive an award. She remained stern and silent, holding her ruler in hand and staring at me as I walked to the front of the classroom. Now I was embarrassed and several little girls made things worse when they began to giggle. The priest handed me a twelve-inch plaster statue of the Blessed Virgin Mary. It looked beautiful in white and pale blue colors. I accepted my reward and began walking back down the aisle to my seat holding my statue at my side. As the class watched, my statue struck a nearby desk and broke. I immediately stopped, and in that long silence, we all listened as Mary's plaster head rolled about the hardwood floor. It was louder than a bowling ball. It was then that all H, E, double L broke loose.

Later, I recall having uttered some words and most likely it did not sound like a prayer. A quick look at Sister Agnes and that triggered an eruption of shrieks of laughter and screams from the class. As old Agnes lunged at me with her ruler, I ran for the back of the class with Attila the Hun in pursuit. Young and scared, I outran her, but as I approached the front of the class the second time around, Agnes cut me off. With no other path left, I bolted past the priest with his mouth still hanging open. Out the door and across the parking lot, I fled for my life—shoestrings and shirttail flying in the breeze. I had cheated death again. Surely, God must love me. Needless to say, the public school system was my next choice of education.

As a young man, I attended many different churches over a period of several years, hoping to find answers and love. The only time that that I heard love mentioned in a church was to advise the congregation that God loves us, even though we were sinful and unclean. There were never any definitive answers or advice on how to find love in our lives. Like so many others, I began to search elsewhere. The organized and scripted approach to religion that had been forced upon me as a child did not satisfy my intellect or my feelings. There was love in my life with my immediate family members, but I needed something more. I chose to look for love, believing that love could be found. Surely, I could find it somewhere. The larger bounds of love that I sought were not to be found as a mental exercise or decision. Still, I wanted to know more of my connection to a creative force and the elegant and mysterious universe. Instinctively, I knew that there must be a way in which I could establish a personal communication with the Creator without the rules of a religious belief system. It was to be many years later that I would discover that it is our expanded human awareness that connects us to the Creator, or the creative universal force.

To this day, most churches of the organized religions keep their secret knowledge from their parishioners perhaps as a matter of control. Over centuries of time, many churches have depended upon their limited theology, ritual, and pageantry to attract and hold the interests of the larger populous. The times have changed, however, and an evolved population now seeks a meaningful, rewarding, ultimate truth. Just imagine how our world would change if everyone, including our elected officials, lawmakers, and teachers were instructed in how to find and share this experience of love.

Recently, I read an Internet news article

wherein the writer described the end of her twenty-year marriage. She reported the realization that her loving relationship and marriage required both parties to work very hard at love. This appears to be a common belief for many people. My experience has been quite the opposite in that my experience of love required no choice or mental decision to participate— love simply blindsided me with a seeming loss of mind. It is often called "love at first sight." My experience showed me that love requires the mind only for the recognition of one's being overtaken by love. The relationship that follows often requires decisions and choices called compromise with the beloved. When we identify completely with the beloved, our own well-being and welfare are then second to that of the beloved and the compromises are very negligible. I am reminded of the words of the Lebanese philosopher Kahlil Gibran, when he wrote that love requires nothing and neither takes nor gives anything but love. Neither does love possess anything nor will love be ever possessed.

Love is the ultimate truth of our existence and that truth is immutable or unchanging. When we explore our human awareness and find our true spiritual being, love will find us. When we seek self-actualization, we can be overwhelmed by a larger transcendent love. At this level of emotional and physical intimacy, the experience of love is best described as a total identification of our self with the beloved. We identify with another to the extent that the total well-being, welfare, and happiness of the beloved is all that we know. When we love unconditionally, we transcend the ego. When we can love without reservation, we need never be concerned about being loved in return. Love then bids good-bye to the ego and fear. Prior to that, it is the ego that creates the largest stumbling block to our relationships and love. There are hardly words to adequately describe the experience of this transcendental love. This acquired state of being is an experience of wonderment, or agape, and includes joy, beauty, peace, and contentment. If and when we can arrive at this experience, all other human emotions are balanced, and fear simply dissipates.

There are many attributes encompassed by love. Consider that we often choose to strive to improve our lives and relationships by practicing intentional acts of love with kindness, compassion, trust, sympathy, and understanding. These acts are virtuous and are a good beginning, but remain ego-driven actions when done because of a mental decision. Sometimes these well-intentioned acts actually become patronizing of the recipient. It is when we are overwhelmed by love and identify completely with our beloved and others, that we do these things quite naturally without the thoughts of consequence. Love transcends the need for compromise. Love is compassion, trust, empathy, understanding, patience, sharing, and many more things that do not require thought. When we act with a loving kindness, it is others who will believe us to be acting thoughtfully. Surprisingly, patience, trust, and fidelity are non-issues in love when we first consider the welfare and well-being of the beloved. When we truly love and care about others, we imagine, or place ourselves in their position and we find empathy, understanding, and actually feel their pain or loss. At this level of love and understanding, we come to know that others cannot hurt our feelings—we hurt ourselves with our own fear, anger, doubt, and mistrust. Others can only provide the situation or stimulus for our own emotional misgivings. Oftentimes our pride gets in the way of loving relationships. Happiness can easily replace egotistical pride. Happiness is a prelude to joy and far more suitable to our realization of our true being. When others are hurtful toward us, it is much easier to try to see through their fear, with love. It is not necessary that we always understand the complexity involved with relationships anymore than we can anticipate coincidence. When we love all of creation, everything appears to be simply beautiful and beautifully simple.

In a universe of energy, we are interactive energy bodies—each connected to, and influencing one another. We are also connected in philosophical and biological ways. A remarkable thing happens when, finally, we come to the point where we love all others. This point comes quickly once we begin to see others on an individual, personal level, much the same way that we see family members. We should learn to see the difference between loving others and not necessarily loving their actions. In this physical–mental world or reality, we were all born equally innocent as perfect spiritual beings.

We have developed relationships with family and friends, with each individual relationship formed on a different level of affection. Our developed human awareness will benefit by an acute awareness of each and every person on an individual basis. Imagine how good it would be to get to know everyone in our lives at a deep, intimate level with an increased mutual understanding. It is our choice.

What is it that happens when passing strangers return our smile? Are we really strangers? What is it that we have in common? The ancient Greeks had a word for this: *philos,* meaning "brotherly love." There are neither the words used to describe the bond felt with others whom we do not really know, nor with those whom we *do* know and love. Why not choose to try to better know those persons who thought to be close to us? Do we afford them enough of our time to visit and really listen to them with interest? Do we truly care and withhold making judgments? We can do these things fearlessly, in love, and when we love them we should tell them so.

In a previous chapter I mentioned an ethereal substance, or plasma, that pervades all things and serves to conduct or carry energies. This transmission of our mind–body energies is powerful and travels the universal ether faster than light speed. The notable scientist, Albert Einstein, found that a lab experiment is altered by the concentrated energy of the lab observer's mind and eyes. *When we change the way in which we see things, we will change the things that we see.* In 1999, a similar discovery was made by the Japanese scientist, Dr. Masaru

Emoto.[6] Experimenting with human thought energies, Dr. Emoto found that when water was exposed to loving thoughts and words, the molecular composition of the water changed to brilliant, complex, and colorful snowflake patterns. In contrast, water exposed to negative energy thoughts formed incomplete, asymmetrical patterns with dull colors. The implications of this research created a new awareness of how we can choose to impact not only our own human bodies that are comprised of more than eighty percent water, but also other individuals and our earth.

Earlier I wrote that, "Where attention goes, energy flows." Our eyes have the ability to direct our thought energies. Likewise, our intentional thoughts are energies, readily sensed by others who are sensitive enough to do so. Perhaps the stranger who returns our smile has sensed our friendly, intentional thought as a greeting. Certainly, you can recall having instantly liked someone upon meeting them for the first time. Do you remember what it was that made you feel that way?

These energy exchanges can be so powerful that many people cannot tolerate or handle the exchange. Perhaps our eyes are the gateway to our soul. Sometimes people cannot afford the personal honesty required or they are seeing others from a cautious, guarded position. I encourage you to take the time and opportunity to sit and look directly into the eyes of someone you love, silently, or while conversing. Watch and feel what happens when you say, "I love you," using only your eyes and your thoughts. There is, obviously, much more to personal communications than words alone, when we wish to provoke love, affection, empathy, and understanding.

In physics, the stronger, higher vibratory energies attract, entrain, and raise the lower energies. And so it is with love. Love begets love and the laws of attraction are always at work. Love and beauty are our inheritance and should be shared. When we become centered in our true inner being, our loving countenance will draw others to our considerate, kind, and compassionate ways. Our family members and children may be the first to benefit by our love. Children are most responsive and they learn what they live with. It is not enough to raise our children in the same manner that we were raised. Children today experience a much more rapid growth and they form their beliefs and behaviors at a very early age. Children readily observe our subtle and intentional energy displays far beyond the spoken word. We should afford them the opportunity to realize their highest potential to levels that took us adults many years to realize. Imagine what this will do to facilitate a global spiritual awakening! Adults, too, will also respond to our example of living in love, compassion, joy, and peace. There is a profound peace and joy that comes from living in accordance with the will of God or the laws of the universe. This personal peace and contentment brings with it our confidence and trust in the natural flow of events and happenings in our lives.

> *The love and beauty that now we see:*
> *This, the ultimate truth will be.*
> —Ed Scott

Life's Purpose

So what has choice to do with our life purpose? *Our sole purpose in life is to realize our inner being—the essence of love.* Actually, finding our true inner being is only the beginning in answering the call to love and beauty. Once we find our inner being or self, we can then ask of the Creator, or the creative universe, "What is it that we should do for the benefit of others in accordance with the will of God or the law of the universe?" Coincidence will quickly bring us the answer. Each of us has a unique set of skills, knowledge, and abilities to fulfill a newfound secondary purpose. Then, coincidence, or a series of unexpected events and choices will appear to show us what we should do. This will bring us the opportunity to begin to live in accordance with our primary purpose of being. We cannot make this happen with our minds and our will power. We can, however, learn to recognize the role brought to us by the synchronicity of events. Once we become aware of our true being and primary purpose, we cannot alter or change that which is happening. Even now, as you read this book, you instinctively know if you have received a gift of grace and are aware of your inner being. You will also know if this information is new to you and that your awakening has not yet begun. Ask of yourself, "Is it my will or thy will to be done?"

Our secondary life activities can now be brought into alignment with our primary purpose. You might ask, "What about raising my children, or dedicating myself to my work? Is this not my purpose in life?" Far too many of us have stumbled along on the path of spirituality for years, with only one foot on the path at times. We have truly believed that these acts were our primary purpose in life, even though time would eventually leave us devoid of our purpose. All of these aspects of a mental purpose are fleeting, or transitory, in a changing world and when they disappear, what then will be left of our purpose? Our children, family, jobs, wealth, and any other external feature that we serve with our mental purpose can evaporate in minutes. Unlike being born-again, a spiritual awakening is not a mental commitment to a belief system or theology. *Our primary purpose in this life is to find and return to our true spiritual being. It is that simple!* When we begin to operate from this level of awareness, we can then see all other actions or activities as a secondary purpose in this physical life. Hopefully, each of us will find a role and secondary purpose that is much greater than ourselves—that of helping or serving others.

Our universe is in constant evolution. Not long ago I listened to a lecturer explain how the world's major societal institutions were failing or disintegrating because of corruption and decline of personal spirituality. Incredibly, all of these changes are occurring simultaneously within the same time period, for the first time in the history of our great country. Perhaps this declination is only a phase in the evolution of our planet. While societal institutions are failing, the personal spiritual growth is increasing. Sometimes a proper balance requires that something must be lost or destroyed in order for us to fully appreciate an improved experience or to seek a return to our primary purpose for being here at this time. Our recent national political campaigns have shown an angry, polarized citizen body and a lack of ethics, integrity, and morality of the mainstream media in investigating and reporting of national events. It is impossible for many people to remain indifferent or even stay neutral and centered in their true spiritual being when subjected to this influence. The human mind, with uncertainty and fear, will drag many people into the folly of arguments and judgments of good versus bad when our society reaches chaotic levels. Beyond a neutral position, we must maintain a positive and active role in assisting others to get through the coming difficult times.

The major world societal institutions presently undergoing degradation include government and politics, commerce and trade, education, agriculture, arts and theater, religion, and societal morality. An entire book collection could be written documenting government corruption, the loss of family farms, unsafe imported foods and products, failing elementary education levels, corporate greed, criminal acts by clergy, and the changing personal moral and spiritual values. According to the U.S. census data, even our national divorce rate is the highest in the world. Some of our country's political candidates have recognized a growing discontent in this country and have promised change for our nation with reforms and new policies.

While writing this book in 2008, I had the opportunity to talk with an Egyptian born woman now residing in the United Arab Emirates. This woman had also noticed a deterioration of American virtue. Having talked with her about the recent economic developments, she related her belief that our country's politicians were the cause of any economic crisis. She further described our present U.S. politicians as operating with deceit, corruption and greed as their Machiavellian creed. Our conversation continued until I mentioned terrorism. The very word *terrorist* was a trigger for the woman to lose her composure and begin an angry rant describing President George W. Bush and all who support him as terrorists. She further challenged me to try and find many Americans who disagree with her view. That was a reality check! The conversation served to remind me to consider her background, education, and her accumulated beliefs to better understand her views and those of many others around this earth. Remembering that energy attracts like energy, or more of the same, it will be interesting to observe what happens within our country and the world in the coming months and years.

Consider that the state of our community and our country is not dependent upon the same factors as are our individual roles.

While our national situation is eroded and suffering, we can enrich our private lives as private individuals. Our reality is exactly what we choose to make of it! Remember that the law of attraction does not distinguish between positive or negative thoughts, but only responds to the energy that we transmit. For each of us, objective reality can be viewed from a neutral state in our consciousness or being. Our state-of-being can be one of indifference with regard to good, bad, positive, or negative. When we are orientated within the natural flow of our universe, national events and crisis will appear very much like those observed while watching a movie or stage play from a neutral state or position. We should continue to be informed but remain detached from emotional distress. It will all work out just the way it is supposed to.

Similar to our personal role, or karma, our communities and our country, each have a role to play in the world theater. Fortunately, there is another aspect of the on-going worldly phenomena; many people in this country are hoping not only for change in many areas, but they are also seeking a meaningful, spiritual resurgence. Change for our country and the entire world will begin with each of us as individuals. It behooves us to begin first with our personal orientation before we think about, or add to the power of a collective energy. Some contemporary teachers and writers refer to this longing for a meaningful life as a *spiritual awakening*. Author Eckhart Tolle[7] eloquently describes how our spiritual awakening is an act of grace and is part of the emerging intelligence of the universe. Others describe a life lived with intention as aligning our spiritual quest with the universal energies. There is indeed, a spiritual awakening happening not only for our country, but with many individuals as well.

Our spiritual awakening and increased spiritual awareness lie beyond our experiences of the physical–emotional realm. The human ego-mind prefers to pursue enlightenment and compares informational enlightenment to that of another person's similar attainment. If you think that you are enlightened, then you are not. If you become aware that you are enlightened, then you will cease to call it enlightenment and you will know that you are now aware of your expanded awareness without measurement. Information and knowledge stimulate our minds, our egos, and our cognitive process, but our human consciousness remains —— awareness beyond thought.

Awakening provides life with a purpose and meaning. Awakening awaits anyone wishing to make profound changes in their life. We need only to take the first step—

go within and identify our true being. Too many of us have been led to believe that as human beings, we should seek a meaningful spiritual experience. The reverse is true. We are spiritual beings experiencing the role of human beings. It is only our human ego that identifies us as something that we are not. Perhaps it is now time to reconnect to our source of being and realize our full human potential. In doing so, we can also find our purpose of being and enjoy a meaningful and rewarding life.

Daily, and hourly, consciously or otherwise, we make choices and decisions—hundreds of choices and many important, sometimes critical decisions. It can be demonstrated that many of our daily actions are routinely made without a large measure of conscious awareness, thought, or deliberate choice. For example, when you awakened this day, did you consciously decide to get out of bed, or was the movement pretty much an automatic one without much thought? Because our dominant thoughts are our future, we should be aware of our thoughts and employ our intention for a particular consequence. We are all entitled to live the life of our dreams and we need only to make the choice. The universe responds to our energies and, in particular, to our sincere gratitude.

Possibly, the single most important decision or choice we can make is to learn more regarding the law of attraction and how to use it to bring change in our lives. It is important to remember the nature of negative energies when making our choices and decisions. If we think negatively about another person, our negativity will not cause harm to that person but will only attract additional negativity to ourselves. When we think in positive terms and language, we create a positive energy environment that attracts only positive choices and alternative choices for our decision-making.

To provide meaningful choices and decisions in our lives, we must prioritize those things that are most important to us. Stop for a moment and think about Maslow's theory of human needs and satisfaction. What is it that we need, cherish, or value the most in our lives? What is it that we wish to change or acquire? Our prioritized changes can be our goals—the precise changes that we will ask for and intend to acquire. We should examine our beliefs and values and then choose the change that we wish to make. To make no choice is also a choice. It often helps to write a list of these things on paper or computer. Will our basic beliefs and values allow us to list spirituality or self-actualization ahead of financial security, or regard our health with a higher priority than service to others? There are an unlimited number of choices that can be made; however, the best choices in our reality will be those in alignment with the flow of universal energies. Once we understand how energies work for us and around us, we can live in the universal flow of a perfect creative force. Our life-altering changes might include an improved health, increased financial security and wealth, loving personal relationships, and a new direction in life with a meaning and purpose. The choice is entirely ours.

> *Believe in yourself, and what you can do,*
> *Value your friends, who believe in you too,*
> *Know yourself and the goals that you pursue,*
> *Your thoughts are your future—your dreams come true.*
>
> —Ed Scott

About the Author

Ed Scott was raised in Minneapolis, Minnesota. He enlisted in the U.S. military after high school and also traveled to Newfoundland, Portugal, Africa, Spain, France, Germany, and England. This gave him an opportunity to observe many cultures and interact with people of differing religions and beliefs.

Upon returning to civilian life, Ed became a police officer with the Minneapolis Police Department where he served for thirty-six years until retirement in 1999. During those years, he attended several different churches for seeking answers and for spiritual growth. Ed is no longer affiliated with any particular faith or worship service.

He has attended several colleges and universities across the country. For more than thirty years, Ed has studied comparative religions, metaphysics, philosophy, and spirituality as they relate to human consciousness and our beliefs. This search led him to become involved with *The Institute for the Study of Human Awareness*, where he served as the board president for fifteen years, until the year 2000. He now lives with his wife in northern Wisconsin.

Ed Scott published *Photo Poems*, in 1985, and *Wisdom of the Heart: Create Your Own Reality*, in 2008.

Bibliography

(Endnotes)

1 Matthew 22:14. New American Standard Bible.

2 Allen, James. *As a Man Thinketh*. New York, New York: Barnes & Noble Books, 1992.

3 Exodus 3:14. New American Standard Bible.

4 John 1:1. New American Standard Bible.

5 Genesis 1:27. New American Standard Bible.

6 Emoto, Masaru, Dr. *The Hidden Messages*

in Water. New York, New York: Atria Books, 2001.

7 Tolle, Eckhart. *A New Earth.* New York, New York: Penguin Group, 2005.